INSTANT CLASSIC

INSTANT CLASSIC

erica kaufman

ROOF BOOKS
NEW YORK

ISBN: 978-1-931824-55-2
Library of Congress Control Number: 2013955367

Cover art by Nicole Eisenman
Untitled, 2012
Monotype on paper, image size: 23 x 17 1/2 in
Courtesy the artist and Koenig & Clinton, New York
Collection of Martin and Rebecca Eisenberg
Photo: Thomas Mueller

Acknowledgments: Some of these poems have appeared in *Little Red Leaves*, *Elective Affinities*, *Parkett*, *Where Eagles Dare*, *The Death and Life of American Cities*, *Lungfull!*, and *Mrs. Maybe*. Sections of this work have appeared in chapbook form from *Least Weasel/Propolis Press* and *Belladonna* (as part of the material lives series). Thanks to the editors/publishers of these presses: Karen Randall, Rachel Levitsky, Emily Skillings, Krystal Languell, and the Belladonna Collaborative.

INSTANT CLASSIC is meant to be a conversation, and this conversation would not have transpired without the support of many people—teachers, mentors, friends, family. Thanks to Wayne Koestenbaum (whose courses gave me the space to write this work in the throes of academia) and Joseph Wittreich (who taught me to love Milton). Thanks also to Sondra Perl, Ammiel Alcalay, Mark McBeth, Eileen Myles, Joan Retallack, Anne Waldman, John Coletti, CAConrad, Matt Longabucco, Tina Darragh, David Buuck, Jane Sprague, Karen Weiser, Carley Moore, Rebecca Brown, Anselm Berrigan, Frank Sherlock, Brandon Brown, Cathy Eisenhower, Ken Jacobs, Charles Bernstein, Stacy Szymaszek, Judah Rubin, Corina Copp, Dana Ward, Thurston Moore, Nicole Eisenman, E. Tracy Grinnell, Charles Bernstein, Simone White, mom, dad, Rebecca, Dan, Isabel, and Bomber.

This book was made possible, in part, with public funds from the New York State Council on the Arts, a state agency.

Roof Books are distributed by
Small Press Distribution
1341 Seventh Avenue
Berkeley, CA. 94710-1403
Phone orders: 800-869-7553
www.spdbooks.org

Roof Books are published by Segue Foundation
300 Bowery
New York, NY 10012
seguefoundation.com

for my parents

INSTANT CLASSIC

PREFACE: to tell you

these forms of beauty have not been to me
as is a landscape to a blind man's lie
("Tintern Abbey" by Wordsworth)

1.

a teaspoon
of ketchup is more
than capitalism important

the problem of how
to read billboards, lawyers,
diction as the experience

of embracing the leeches.
i don't control my own
metaphors, humanized

amputation a straw taken
to the puss of the road.

2.

if she never photographs
the hair on the mirror
i'll wear the face

of upright lamentation
half fixed melancholy
half i can still sidestroke

and say, *you need to have awe*
to be mercenary. or, *look at me*
as if you are grooming a tree.

Instead of an Argument

AFTER THE FIRST edition of *Paradise Lost* (1667) proved itself to be far too difficult to be a bestseller, John Milton's publisher, Samuel Simmons, asked the author to give his readers a little help. The result of this is seen in subsequent editions of the epic—in twelve books instead of the original ten, and with short prose arguments that precede each book. This shift from Milton's original text to a more palatable publication, one that is geared towards consumption, is what initially drew me to epic, to *Paradise Lost,* to feeling troubled by the connotations of prelapsarian time.

There was never a place for me in the garden. And, despite Milton's clearly planned entry into this traditional form, it seems as though there wasn't really a place for him either. In "The Verse" (one of the sections added post-1667 edition), Milton writes, "The measure is English Heroic Verse without Rime, as that of Homer in Greek, and Virgil in Latin; Rhime being no necessary Adjunct or true Ornament of Poem or Good Verse." The tone here clearly articulates Milton's knowledge of the epics that he is following, and gestures towards ambivalence towards the act of composing a statement titled "The Verse." What does it matter who is reading?

In *Areopagitica*, Milton writes, "hee who destroyes a good Booke, kills reason it selfe." Published in pamphlet form in 1644, this document pre-dates Milton's forays into epic, and i can't help but wonder if there is some connection between epic and censorship—between "extreme amounts of writing" and the "suppression of speech." *Paradise Lost* is "extreme" in its composition and content—and i mean this as a compliment. As Joan Malory Webber writes, "*Paradise Lost* balances creation against destruction at the center of its pattern... heroic endeavor only occurs because men are fallen." In the *Genesis* rendering of Adam and Eve, we see man being "made" and then "placed" in the garden. Milton introduces us to man already fallen—a hard "in medias res" image for the human exceptionalist, narrative story craving readership to embrace.

Who owns language? Is language a body to liberate? Milton was undeniably not the most palatable of literary figures—publishing radical texts on both censorship and divorce in a time when that was not the genre of discourse one engaged in. In 2012, i am reluctant to name myself, to give in to the egotism that might be inferred from wanting to lie alongside John Milton. But, i am a woman, a lesbian, a Jew. In my daily routines, it is perhaps easier, within academia (or my version of academia) to not exist. i pass. i can pass. sometimes i choose to pass.

But, wait, this is my way around a preface to a "difficult book." i needed to reckon with Milton, to feel empathy for the way Samuel Simmons changed the capitalizing of his name from edition to edition, to really think through what it means to have an "argument" with both book and self. But, wait, i think i mean to welcome you to *INSTANT CLASSIC*.

INSTANT CLASSIC is the phrase that trailers use to promote a film that is "certain" to be a blockbuster hit. *INSTANT CLASSIC* is the term that some men use to describe a certain portrait of a certain woman in which she looks unusually (or unexpectedly) striking (in the traditional sense). *INSTANT CLASSIC* is the term i always seem to want to grapple with—and i imagine that my grappling might somehow run parallel (or diagonal) to Milton's tongue-in-cheek "The Verse," that my grappling might be a way to redeem the *Paradise Lost* of 1667, when there were no "Arguments," where the text was allowed the plain it wanted to occupy.

erica kaufman
10.31.13

I

"And now the time in special is, by privilege to write and speak what may help the further discussing of matters in agitation."

(from *Areopagitica* by John Milton)

"Meanwhile Satan alights upon the bare convex of this World's outermost orb; where wand'ring he first finds a place since called the Limbo of Vanity;..."

(from *Paradise Lost*, Book Three
by John Milton)

INSTANT CLASSIC

without asking the chariot
i walk towards the scene
first interest leave. be it eve
in the garden voiceless
or a moment of heterosexual
panic that necessitates it
necessary to dive plural drive

how true is the Milton
you suggest. how long
your internal construction
of warfare, your satire of the men
in the sky. be it norm or kin structure.
hair cut or handmade satchel.
your army is no match for

my stairs. waif. behemoth.
spinal amalgamation. the metal
in my neck stronger than any
revisionist fantasy of Pocahontas.
i am stronger than your
"perfect humanity" your arch-
angelic plates reminiscent

a moment of general anesthesia
translate to mean antithetical
to missing you o, lax inhibitor
don't diet until derive
on wig shanty, thus the want
to be cowboys, not mothers.
posthuman, not interlocutor.

INSTANT CLASSIC

always riding we look back to the image of the tiger
predominantly stoic but necessary, like being in cahoots
with the experience of power and amputation.

politically retrograde but still the story
of perfect humanity, dateline pornography,
the fortunate fall as crucial as opting

for an artificial ankle, or a way of changing
the terms of who we're looking at. don
the clothes of the apocalypse and take

the typical vision of a woman nodding,
see a dragon, and name religion war.
amidst all this new world analog,

learn to speak the language of bodice
ripper, then idealize the valley, birds replaced
by sepulchers, use "man" as a verb.

INSTANT CLASSIC

for/after Tina Darragh

we can't all be ballerinas, ducks, or robots
and we can't all heed the ventriloquist and live
in the apothecary's store indulging in mercury,
tobacco, the occasional pomegranate reminiscent
of models of rupture, but i can't be
responsible for what places look like
in a world where the word *reverent* is so deeply
political and turtles are walked on a leash

if the man on the subway was just a man on the subway
if the only words we hear are "ambiguous salvation"
if we no longer have the capacity to be human   make love
if one can never know who is mad, who is Promethean,
perpetual adolescent, dovetail, scarred landscape
surveillance i will cite you if i only if i only had
an ecosystem of buzz words, a hairnet full
of intellectual property, a patent on spinster

as a means of introduction (translate to mean trade
secret) artificial like peer-to-peer botany public
domain vision quest rights i am sharing right
i am sharing all rights   pictionary this   meta-
topiary Steamboat Willie prosthesis ensnared
in moot neutrality and chalk it up to *if the work*
is a work for hire and um yeah i call this "all things
digital" or the "Luke Arm Tango"...fairy use, k?

we can't all be bionic commonwealth sundries, suntanning
worried about the source list of the day compulsory
sic contrapuntally sic the reproduction of public faces sic

in thy voice, digital watermarking, retrieval capacity duplex
in thy voice an enormous price tag a shopping bag
a frozen foods concession a victim of the familiar victim

we can't all be fasting and feasting and fasting and fleeting
innovative in the usual carnage mode the language of
"i agree with you" afloat in some vast bowl of Jell-O
somewhere where i am very much the valevictorian,
cloverleaf, composition, unprotectable and we, the olympic
particular, annoyed by having to greet Wonderwoman
nouveau Edenic epoch tenor bad magician waif

INSTANT CLASSIC

after Jane Sprague

(A)
with the advent of an airbrushed leg
elementary in its images of skull caps
piety and rosary'd   scars accurate

as the liturgical want to roll over and be
docile   think it is not so hard to
imagine what the carnival looks like

a loveseat of intertextuality a struggle
with water resolved in the non-site
non-space nonsense panel of ugly

models who salute the body in all its
metabolistic habitation push for—

(B)
Let us go find growth and evaluate them. Let the gentrification of gangster movies symbolize the true possession of time. Let the rhetoric of *how* become the quest for new media copyright collage or just papers crumbled then splayed on the floor. The pedagogy: a container or an additional link to babycages.net. Another quasi-consumerist bunny-lovin' frond.

(C)
I believe there are some archives that are ecstatic
more expansive (expensive?) than the head of a mascot

or the catalog of syllables in the telegraphist's hand
an athletically presenting intelligibility cold rinse cycle
admit I find myself timid effaced or in the face of

the posthuman variable techno-activism

belief that "denying the lover who thinks" is
a manifestation of commodity   and translate

"lover" to mean ipod   "thinks" to mean play
in virtual feelie-suits data gloves tiny sex in vital

how long will it take the man in a can
to seem normal again bookended by biochips

a boat a float amidst the taste of concentrate homo—
economic anarcho-heart cum antennae

(D)

In 1960 the first cyborg was a chimp in space. The grand science of dildonics had yet to be publicized. We still drew with pen and paper, saw a deer as a deer, not part train. We spoke to each other, wrote letters, and never thought of polymers as an integral part of social graces.

I admit not to be afraid of my semi-object state. My first swimming lessons were from an amputee.

Extended Release (para- INSTANT CLASSIC)

1.

what was meant to be the stomach
becomes the mouth and today's chic
is just another way into   leprosy
this organization of thinking.

so let's take the farmer's market under-
ground. suppress the fight-or-flight
response to pork plants, de facto
finger-thumb theory vampirized
versus consolidation—call "dinner!"

i have no apologies for a lack of blood.
i take my provisional self by the sternum,
deem it Latin for "zombie of any inclination."
I've no qualm that a spleen infection
is not censorship or a function of anarchy.

rather, "the body in tact" is a proverb
for postmodern studies, gourmandism,
a happening of the progressive kind.

2.

data thrashing
schizoid lumberjack
slap the machine
on the back
crack the ol'
imperativism ask
to dose or not to dose?
for circulation is
the Rite Aid i want
so bad got me some
cartel fever some
simpatico panache
freshly waxed no
longer dependent
on the usual ankle
bracelet prison bling
mild name drop
wanna reference?

3.

it is not a moment
of necessity it is not
raining anymore
for the moment it
is not the rip
on the side of my
galoshes or it is
not the want
to be heard but rather
a craving for a specific
accent that gloriously
mispronounces migraine
recognizes solicitation
with a call-out box
labeled blunt elbow
jab pants ride hi
on the screen
of my pleasure

INSTANT CLASSIC

o suffuse recognition of Objects
strictly theoretical, a roguery efface
peri-familiarization   urban surgery
          rather recalcitrant
                    children's methodological
approach to majesty one of many savage
rhetoricians who sing
          all you need are goats
                    or a sensibility change pyramidal
evanescent in inherent linearity
first person feral or the historiographic
nonchalance stage of sub-reflection

o unmodified Object aggregate
contractual canine empath please barter
neo-cortex style, take the dead-man's self-portrait
to be the most confusing time of our passage
          contextless with a disdain for mastication
immune to the tinkerer's generic virus which places
introspection in lace
                              bodice position aptitude
                              substantive   *arrest it*
monochromaticizing
                    the problem with the man is
electronically postconstant pigeon-esque anemone
choose to be or to deliver selective industry

o Object analogue utterance
o new spatial abjection, superannuated
name effect fluid as the difference
between *is* and envelops careful

suit of the self   brain-fag protagonist tweed
matriculation phantasmal vocabulary
of namelessness accuracy of not this leg
ether overtone the ratio between resolve
to become and resolve to mulch
                    gut-feeling with suprathreshold
                    we don't dine on mammals with let's wait
duplicate the edible plants   her office   the plate

o to the woman who keeps falling out of grass
o Object emblem of the anti-Washington Irving moment
where instead of talking about Milton we gather and be Milton
together speak in tactile verse using only words
like "scary" "warranted" "fixation" among other
phrenological ditties culled from only
                    the finest filigrees numerous
                    in mullet country
the so-called reservoir a single harvest heartless
like the lone emu lone alpaca amongst the biblical
marching band progression o want to reside

INSTANT CLASSIC

no honeymoon lasts forever, honey
because you gotta git on the plane
plunge into the paleomagnetic dating
pool
                                        with your searchable self
misrecognised for what it is—

                                                        house hunger
                                                        vogue terms
                                                        liturgical abject

in mullet country euphemisms
are advocacy and your wrist
overhauled like the hypothesis

of uptight walking, urban implosion
the new therapeutic—
                                                        super bank
                                                        threshold theory
                                                        we can scream

let's make the machines
who make other machines
download the same filter
totally *kumbaya* every second

and split the risk of being
a social agent composite
of real churches

                                        a way to save space
                                        in the closet of valence

where convention equals

hot biographical impasse
like everyone's going to remember
you as photogenic

a vatic practitioner
too small a nuisance
please

INSTANT CLASSIC

our brain works by filling in locations
infer snobbery or the moonwalk of synesthesia
where a rehearsal of odorama leads to
primadonna something planetary
a gestalt experience
paradigmatic of the boundaries
of processing ideas absent
rather proof of a proclamation
silent letter articulate as Tinkerbell
in her position as professional mourner
tutu and all disambiguous mercuric
captioned performative device creature

creature performative device captioned
her idea process absent
                                        articulate
                                        disambiguous
in its rehearsal of mourning
positions and moonwalk locations

amidst mixed reception we can't bear
the autodidact in fashion
actor interaction doppelganger aesthete
tie me to the bar representing coordinate time
second-order petri magnet all micro micro
and unsanction this posey genetic itch

INSTANT CLASSIC

we are all mutants in our own gaze
relapsing into false memory syndrome
symptomatic of the urge to become
a thing destroyed a trumpet
for the past another plastic
object encapsulates movement
encapsulates convention equals
plot to convene our cochlear selves
so the body becomes general
practitioner compartmentalized
the kind of retrograde that affects
all things physical the apparatus
less glamorous more barbaric sprawl

but we are already civilized people
social agents manipulated
by the vast potential of mishearing
an escort and a dowry typically
doused like the *i want to get used*
to how the elite live or mark
impoverishment as luxury like
coffee, soda, and other elements
of delivery genetic or *hi there,*
make sure you put your body
in the right space

we begin in birth we witness
legacy applicants visibly invisible
advisable the tip of a flat
belly the self-hypnosis hypothetical

this may be a joke coincidence
a powerful optimism download
up-speak the "neurotic character"
white-out situation proteus figurine that
means *congrats* you're finally in vocation

INSTANT CLASSIC: TYPOS/SLIPS

i don't believe in criminal justice

i know she only jumps when she can
play the martyr card, wear all black,

and run from the economic humiliation
of walking into a room with swollen

lips scored by the root of the tooth
that falls out I can't get a password

past-poor of import i never turn

on my ringer gyrate grate the waste
remember the instructions

are the test the best logic
of impounding details de-rail to repeat

precisely you must do more

than just observe dentures in action
enjoyably aphasic i know the time

will come and i will pick the bus
harness the pirate remember it is only

arthritis in the eye only the same
tissue as the knee suburbanized

old-mobile if the word strategies
is spelled correctly use the term

like a consultant an ear trumpet
at last romanticize the root that snows

shows intubation cross country
lung collapse some semblance of what

i used to be before i got all third
generation medi-can't mobile in all

the right papers authentic a constitution
age or a meatloaf between the tears

there is nothing wrong

with looking in the mirror a tendency
for the simulator to work badly

i have to *do* my career

to have a total gustatory experience
to be eligible for deductions

to admit the reception purposefully
bad because *you know*, she says,

you know we don't matter and
i leave this place always taped

in hand handcuffs on metallic stud
bikini petro-glad this elevator

used to be broken, *thanks*
i'm gonna clothes on green

it's always got to be about pattern

INSTANT CLASSIC

in the virtual workplace facial
recognition hinges   on assembly,
penalty free motivation, and
the introduction of public toys
define happiness as anti-solidarity
never just a body, but a body
with noise
                                it isn't so depressing
if you think of an actual snowman
doing it, an affirmation
of the adoption curve

there's more than just a single flag
over there, prognostications only take us
so far so let's do it again, with a limp
this time dignifying the repetition
of unknown female unknown

•

i don't buy passion theory
natively good at two-way modernista
communication describe all painting

as a problem with cognition, see
you gotta race war(s) and be her
know the definition of capable
like, "remember, capability brings you
here." you can't say anything
about us   you can't say anything
not about us
a tribute is not that different

from a meeting house
never sure where the bench breaks

•

who knows what fascination really is
the people formerly known as audience
need to know resonance
                                        is superficial
a form of lingering in parameter
or another business and i am just
less disguised another kid who sits
down and makes commercials

in order to find my own voice
in the dressing room of compassion
i try on then tailor the cheerleader
machine opting out of transparence

remember, we all drink the same kool aid
give bibles as gifts, harbor brand fans
in the formulaic thermos of uncharity

stir   offer traditional capital return
acupuncture to chosen cause

II

"I leave you to choose whether a factory is nicer or more liberating than a theater."

(from *Revolt, She Said* by Julia Kristeva)

"Because my body is not seen as a mere object by me, I necessarily have a different relation to it than to any other objects."

(from *Volatile Bodies* by Elizabeth Grosz)

INSTANT CLASSIC: transition, a formality

there is nothing unique or historical
about a traffic jam there is nothing
quite like forced conversation

in real life we don't talk long
without interrupting
that is nothing   unique historical

conglomerate how you monetize
the library shelve tiny acts of protest
alongside anemic conversation

dolly back to *mayor at the movies*
type error choreograph campaign placards
emblazoned with nothing unique nothing hysterical

because we don't apologize anymore at least not
in public the new epistemic shift to
lifelong bachelor forced conversation

in megalo-dialectic sing forgive
the accuser forgive the sponsor
quiet like a record of conversation
where nothing is historical

INSTANT CLASSIC (homo)retro

1.

how many times can we be clandestine
repeat clandestine repeat the open marriage
agenda penetration and think about all
the switch-boards human, agile, an interpretation
of the sherpa we all hold inside the masculine

voice can only summarize foreign films
and other moments where heterosexist
observation slows down as if it is visibility
that's portent the privilege of virility
a register of upper class escapism anti-
binary dancing and so i say—

"my physical gifts are no use"
economic military mimicry where city
state just another body's network device
deep like religion and money and back
when i was your aim and dialed into it

and you remind me of a horse a self-maintained
costumer whose pants are what does
all the work the fluff of the loss war excess
out of excess out of excess out of air
take wristband take nails take parameter

2.

let's say i can visualize my own film
build a public garden out of body
language index the utterance devoid
of spokespersons who use *faggot*
for affirmative because it is more
than just shacking up with liberatory
ideology the larvae that fucks
everything i'm not sure i want to be

transparent anymore a new species
that doesn't hold a model of my story
doesn't write *epic fail* on my hypothetical
strive to be beautiful new department installed
the first time i thought about that word
seriously couldn't look beyond my own palate

3.

in this narrative i market myself as "generally happy" and carry a pill box that stays the same. we are all elements of epic sometimes like the antique who really belongs to the man that lives here and cries and channels machines like i count outlets cross diamonds raise glasses every five hours. this is the way to get around that academic stage, where there is no chance to rehearse plenary or to assume we'll get to a movie and find an usher or another person writing this form thriving requires more than just survival.

INSTANT CLASSIC: a crown

the succession of syndromes   the recital bias

the meta-context   the economic colloquy

the coffee cup the mouse my fantasy of tea

drinking then wrangling donkeys the pretense

collage because stains always hold what

immense meaning and only the parotid

oblige a new way of talking about the heart

known as greed and i say let's plant

vegetable garden aesthetics in the shunt

of every front lawn a blue ocean opportunity

pocket sundial   corporate sage rotation

repeat   we imagine corset structures speech

perception discriminative like drawings of

luxury a model exercise in boning to stay place

say place a model luxury a boning exercise
an acknowledgement of the difference
between naked and nude self-irrelevant
or the text that i have when i go home
and resurrect the pigeon that shits
in cleavage the bared breast a symbol
of wean   necessary schism share a past
around my neck with the conductor
who i wear like medical discourse tight-lace
workhorse   we facilitate tourism pretend
we don't travel alone   the epic split
between *action* and *contemplation* a body
art ally half expecting a discussion of
striptease   only breathe the top my lung

and so we breathe   stripped easy lung excess

reminds us to act as good men do   revert

to wilderness trope   this time with tagline

bring a hatchet a geographic whore   regular

elated but still standing her face   a shrine

to the resurgence of guardianship   refined

missing teeth   successful   detached

a great day in the forest   figuratively

center my chaos   desire polynomic

self-similar metafunctional piggybank

allegory for *we are going backwards* and

i have no place to talk amidst all this ideal

geometry   collective *tell me* through risky

fool escort   middle this   plural flight

escort plural nights of middling faces
what does it mean   to no longer cry
in testimony   a public obsessed but this
is not a tragic story   not another situation
i want to read but can't   arborescently
listening to programs of limbs extending
from windows their veins my athletic
periphery a work in progress a caricature
of daily bread   i transcribe the work
a whole regime of roving of putting down
the hearing aid proficiently demonic a city
kid severely upholstered to prevent
something ugly   old-hat   instead live in
gallery walks   casebook fjords   divorce

casebook divorce gallery   walk floored well
turn your head   loose in the library
where i tell myself stories about vikings
the importance of audio pirates   bathtubs
declawed   people love constraint some
partial to laboratory ideal qualities of down-
time the permission never to use words
like "limbo"   "balance"   "vanity"
all talismanic invitations for signage
protection in the form of bras and panties
ascend out of the captioned "she"   a new
balance between raffle tickets and propaganda
between the tip of a cliff and the face
gracious dictatorial not in compliance

gracious when compliant   dictatorial not
typical create a plaza with a fountain confuse
oil on birds with big media breech lethargic
we all know this is not history we all know
a pelican serves as signpost   argue success
in closure   monetized   abject as orientation
my imaginary safety net democratic   romanticized
behest   a balcony scene because i can bracket
use railings   cliffs   deploy my own figuring
as circled word   i am   up   here   she   is
speaking   about the lament we all   grasp
revision of tonsils as markers   a logo-thetical
bridge between audience and dead heroic see
there are lizards her menagerie we ride them

in this menagerie there are lizards so i ride again
build a boundary across arguments for similarity
conditional like   "she is also called a throat"
or "this doesn't look good in address" afraid
of bodies   utter   hip to a code   to the code
i can now   throw overboard   husk reticence feed
no images no longer skirt a need to   evoke "she"
one less arrow in the quiver waning and by that
the self-censor   the blank android   the t-shirt
i used to want to wear too much   and say
"what's chosen constrains me" in deep intent
robot voice   florid   like "this is the peacock
and her undoing" a distraction can't be
depicted on stage   ectopic   feather pulse

originally she imagines a department store awake
congruent to this concept of journey   water-related
retail open as the form   a crown a framework
for landscape where she pulls herself into the ark
returns a litany of hands a rubric to gauge
familial styles of man both barber and fighter
gouge the suitcase and find the real question
that begins "maybe if i take enough photos"
interrupted as inadequate because we are sharks
to each other and she's a shark again but
there's no room for animals now this narrative
she can't speak and so falls a lapse into
accessible gesture drawings a system to act
as she drives through her body endorsing alone

feather ectopic   pulses on stage depict fictive
like you can choose your family your flashlight
your connection to the pothole pitfall
compost psychosis   i know this introduction
public body confused recyclable chant
"my operation cannot be by chance" or
"let's give eden night" wedded imagined
the job is the implant control to control
to loop homeric   google prosthetic body
language be a narrative   alter this mouth so
my face is not a face not a place synthetic
i collect companions like ringtones   tradition
badly   admit there are problems in the landfill
robotopic cyborg construction   not stable not self

not cyborg self not robotropic staple construction
not dinosaur cyclops a canine dream   voodoo
economic a corroboration between the voice
through speakers and the lantern i wear
across my sternum recharge a need to
collapse missing piece into multiplication pathos
her sound my sound recur repose receive
response   from more vultures more sky burials
tweed blazers i need to herd carnal coast
past she to i to a moment to bray and declare
this is not my genre of testimony   provocateur not
my signatory i'm not troubled   by this body
because naming now *my* choice a gift a blouse
a silent play a mutual mime   my metric theater

play mime theater through silence metrically
relevant yet the map is language disowned
i build a stairwell in her doorway a template
state for shoulders unwanted fleshy the torso's
trailer ostensibly mobile built of a branch hung
whole body epic imaging it hurts not to open
the window but who can say malfunction genie
wing negative   queen fragile   integrity gene flight
airport blacklisted like wave scenes pass the ark
its masculine expense of water where i don't get
to pick and choose   obliterate our condition blatant
market text majority   i'm pursuing my actual
house a desert versus rainforest sexual incident
retort   picture compatible uniform course

uniform retort compatible   picture a horse

is not my totem   i don't want travel to arrive

fertilize through dedication to find pride

in drone my neck too strong for all the obvious

pollen please make me hand over my tail pre-

predatory a certain reflection of the penny's

visage not wanted on this voyage where i

spread my insurance out razor style akin

to the inner boar   she speaks through me

air-ports wave scene barium scavenge high

temperature swallow inner-metallic vacuum

my throat permanent white with the challenge

to keep a breast any breast an alloy of gossip

x-rays worry screenings precious fluids finally say

finally say worry is precious   x-rays fluid
bluff scares me a mess to clean up later
where there is a there there   abstract
as tolerator or in the sense where we all act
as parasites and i find another whale in
this moment of vocalizing i know i author
memory in question find the animal giraffe
flavor of standards the second hand stress
of who   is   she   stealing for   the lesson
plan wants   out   wants to privilege
the other as idea malingering legacy industrial-
made graphic she doesn't envy science she
doesn't soft wear she don't test performance
code paint a widow open the throne

window code throne a performance open
skylight rain down on the stone it grows
important prepared to thwart walking off
without first leading the climb down
learn to fine the polygon auto-complicate
and remember the she is i now and the i
not done by computer like her likeness
commuter devolve sequential reruns she
over i am the one who only who always sees
the gorilla inside a circle an epic example
of why speech no longer fleets but feeds
on all that distribution training i get
the mountain global   recreation is not
a pursuit but the claiming my gravatar

now claim this pursuit endorse my body
gravitate towards a model of luxury plural
not silent throne monger stage robot mime
precious because these x-rays were my uniform
now a window open a lizard walks alone
i am not sacrificial here her garden envy mounting
counterfeit repentance blackout screenings skylight
circa the bindings the binges the proximal node
code for the i is a woman who finds comfort
in logistics knows we'll all be famous in some
windshield these stories regenerate shift happens
when i get affidavit split rinse explain as if i could
how our illness presents me a parasol in one hand
ordering of syndromes bias meta map the other

INSTANT CLASSIC: help me i'm regressing!

there's another version of this story
where i am a man my concerns a bible

where i luxuriate in authority despite
water aesthetics & i say "it doesn't

always have to be this hard" & believe
it.   in this story my rib cages bungled

my hush voice irrelevant because i can
repeat the word any word any   into

public light interrupting the dogs
that train me   conceal   hard i rant

to impress not to cope not to echo-
locate face the reinvention committee

the prospect of bronzed bodies easy
Vitruvian etched proportionate one

foot in each crow recursive as shit
in this story the real center my navel

the human body depends on more
than just the position of fins   legs

a part of the voice we only deepen
over time find a viable pastime in

anthropometrics a way to optimize
my skull products occipital prospectus

mine a signal origin single in this story
i do have a fingerprint   it matters

•

so let's hang the used condom on a branch
of an olive tree   let's ask one less question

at the end of each chapter   & read
"float alone and singing" my skeleton

into this new legal setting where tear gas
reminds us of the carefree days of simple

constitution worship in this story i wear
the same face as the serpent flushed

with genuine potential or the desire to return
the womb to my own version of Isaac ramrod

genital sprouting from insistence   in this
story i show compassion for the man outside

the logic of altar state   where a garden
makes sense   where equine resembles angelic

speech   my documentary hypothesis one
paragraph repression in this story we don't care

about my hero's sorrow nature   her apology
editable   a portion of scripture where

animals make sense as substitutes for what
is voice the same type of narrative platform

guild of the perfect   legally merely inspired
in this story we're all humiliated on his
mountain   we're all a defining movement
that bears no filial import   machetes & the detail

save us   teleologic locker room perpendiculars
recreate the romantic today   predator done

INSTANT CLASSIC: a[tone]meant

1.

don't be sick anymore don't sit
silent   recliner mute to the suit
that earns me political return look
through that window only slightly
mutter verbs like persuade, probe,
phrenology, fellow, transgress against
that diaphragmatic urge to be again
"that girl" time marked by shoe sizes,
length of hair   instead propose a practice
a fishbowl where the eye a woman
and the rain really does help
            us avoid the boat the impulse
to just move some chairs around
say "jigsaw   my framing device"
and no longer thirst for genuine
saltwater connection epic armor
i knew i was naked i got off the ark

2.

shift happens the drowned drown i find
comfort in how my illness presents me
peripheral   my political skirt   sewn
savor   hang it   on the mast of
generationality   caption: eve dreams
in her garden   caption: this isn't the way
i taunt authority hoard pillow tape
tea bags stain residual creativity i wear
pearl necklaces   in place a scarf
a parsing parody tailgate   parity
ballroom the many reasons why
the epic draws me   in full situ
the armor it used her vocal gait
reenter the vice state interpretive fame
shift from "i   the intended person" to
"i am the body that brings theory back"
and this metaphor works   even in riot
gear   transferrable i don't buy into easy
queer expletives the common core pressure
of how to handle analysis amidst all these
worries of dress codes worries read no
cardinals warnings wary i wear "questionable
disciple" on my aisle seat resist some
conglomerate effusion fresh blood
duct tape truncheon i won't appropriate
this body won't seat myself in face

3.

awake i need to superimpose my other meditate we *are* mediated media point one point one point to won out put as awareness the intersect shuns my face images the typical hero never

sees a baton trust glass door verti-gone it's actually not that easy to be horizontal to stage a sit-in a ring bearer a circus circumvents the marital process camera as narrator as "she is genuinely distraught" becomes traditional design

no more no invitation to transparency costume as crouched again again we don't see her face the angle of entrance blocking rather the rhetoric of garden breech imagine handcuffs on the fruit of his tree

in a former light i a rattlesnake shape shift swamp rockets you owe me shame and a basket of flowers you owe me more than the typical snake guardian mythography pathogenic technology fails us

bacteria fills images the protagonist never sees aphids notorious sapphic gene transfer a host range of facial mismanagements socially registered turnstiled i used to occupy and harbor i used to wish for a reception marketed

a way to get home count the penguins on the lake geese that fly down ground myself in a need to feel pre-lapsarian if you observe your right generic if you accept me crass and secret keeping

the one who says "i don't know how to chant" and "i can't recognize crowd" so join me for a moment of clothing imagery that breaks all leaf-life salutes to terminology always supplicant a tentacle to extend from apple to branch to the base of my fee every house of cards needs a queen to collapse a flag not flying because we're all part of a machine we don't easily assume everything lately everything i do purposefully dramatic

like i can't sleep alone can't handle a male voice raised and i want to write a formal essay where we're all in the garden again topless melodic tattooed with the mark of real harrow feral i write

the autobiography of the talent i've never met who allowed me to be this vulgar in my relationship my rendering of insomnia i just don't want sleep

4.

i am the technology that fails us
i am the person that went to the meeting
i am a woman and a woman and a bulldog

admittedly belligerent paranoid
all the right days involve
both the garden and the closet

i am the dead centipedes our synthetic windpipe
i am the tattoo you cover with a gun
i am the place that offends me attraction hunter

remember it is possible
to lose your fingerprint
then make it official

i am the anti-hagiographic emo-bibliography
i mark my chest with wings sociogrammatic
i am where you are on the rubric at least

for another minute
sometimes seeming inarticulate
is okay productive content transplant

i am confused about inheritance and manners
i am polylingual reclaim the term “bitches” as positive
i fold my body between “birthright” and “eliminate”

but the word across my temple
“assimilate”   pass   remind
refine

i am not the reason speech stops
i am not part of the decision that attracts attack
i don't remember how to find my way again

from the market once out in the street
physical trapped some climb
and assimilate i learn to knit

i am the snake outside your history
i am far from archaic from scaffold repositories
i am vulgar in my fear of impact and inflation

success a woman in beta
launch jitter epic reputation
total comments allowed =
hear the territory
then reframe it

INSTANT CLASSIC: {well fare well}

it isn't fun anymore to wake
half-scratched lip corner
cracked wide iron deficit
knee roiled i put on my best
embargo qualifier and do
very little about objects
and infection glamouflaged
as capstone comfortable in my
own question fidelity dude mecca

grammar waist i am not
obsessed that word signifies
problem gluten gunpowder retinal
detach men instead embrace
the eye extropic frozen identify
one real garden one man
and his own flood always
impulsive evidence trashed

let's thrash against typical
engagement against foot soldiers
shoutbox movie of the mind
trailers tailor what i know
to epic feverishness episodically
inappropriate like the saga
of the man who exposes himself
over and over and i'm allowed
only in that tent weapons spent

debt led leave me stuck here
green thumb overt heroic so
i scratch my forearms temples

my one attempt to prove *no*
one is looking at you no one
clumsy feeble vulgar volatile
serial it is my voice that narrates
primaries an acumenical fall

like thinking about body economy
reptile breadth dominos we recess
like cities and it's the burden
of a burden of my bank noise
apparitional hypochondria perceived
exertion but today we don't talk
conceptual focus on the fiscal
gender phantom account for
the difference between flashback

and origin story essential idealism
i'm not having a moment yet
where i pretend to ask for approval
and hunt for the legible and lasting
desire to be in cahoots with any faculty
because i don't sit here i don't have
an audience an office an offer
an officer a full audit of real

crowd experience i begin hyper-
logical at war in my own garden
hospice where it's the wheelchair
who guides me from tree to tree to
anemic courting rhetoric entourage
i'm attracted to the question
of attraction decorative in utility

wallflower board-game   new journalist
subversive wallow   pick the translator
who sees thee

III

"By one man's disobedience lost, now sing
Recovered Paradise to all mankind"

(Milton, *Paradise Regained*, The First Book)

"Let me recite what history teaches. History teaches."

(Gertrude Stein, "If I Told Him")

INSTANT CLASSIC: (re)genesis

1.

i would like the apple to talk to us to encourage
the feminization of this surveillance   state-imposed
pathway   to active verbs you force repeat as in the epic
cycle of remediation a ward that translates toxic state
toxic i bear fruit   it's rotten   my idea vacation
some project   a view   in my exile realize my identity
always a problem my lineage street cred proportional
my history develops to fit the face the tumor steroid
chemo cancer goiter dis-ease genetic narrative strait
dance party petri dance horseshoe kidney fever sprite

remove a part of my body   stitch me   switch my blood
type to anesthetic   pierce my nipples then wake to
reject the metal   expel   neuropathetic
a littoral accounting of every   time i change
my self to be some one else   put it on
cake walk   genocide dreams   where the snake
no more a symbol than the pallor i see when
i sleep just the right amount   of disheveled
alongside my character   she represses longing
regresses back into the suitcase sermon compendium

coda for i'm always in pose in public state
always preoccupied compensate for photography
in this parking garage of illegal places i'm used
to life in trauma to posturing care giver care
taker but i don't know how to take care to increase
parallelism to get my self out of the conservatory
and into the well where i can be the enamored
tourist embracing "berate me" as unilateral carnage
fail promissory rote i'm not over mountain aloof
hoax maelstrom object listen misread complaint

compliant listen when i tell you parade is key
our place is under the highway where we wear
our surface reissue ballot measures foreclose
on the participatory gleam of pink slips decisive
ledge trademark contingent laborer tax monkey
ugly mantra desultory death toll tour extreme-proof
i was born in this vocabulary of basketball
sleeves wrist brackets morphine pagodas
two happy meals and the woman i see every
morning in secrecy in dictum in perfume

initially feel like tangent initially lopsided
in the vest of indulgence initially private
my vision of sibling rivalry initially peak-housed
a precipice mount for radiological panic it's not
a funeral i see out instead instances fainting
a plethora of mornings where my bed an MRI
my archangel say nothing and the camel eats
of every tree so i let the wicked touch me let
nakedness become a chore let wearing a form
of uniform become a way to bray witness

2.

of course i turn to salt of course i turn
around rub mud on my face   pray
light don't reflect back   do damage to
cheek bones   mark me   elegiac i know
about the looting the plunder the silver
furniture future   if this is true   democracy
please invite me   to the meal that follows

in the sepulcher in the archway in the cloister
closing closet closer   i'm trouble   by desire
i co-opt "come out"   it is not good for man
to be alone   of course i want to name home
this place   wounded people   where hair grows
on statues and lethal injections bring us closer
my former self dressed in figs   don wings
a robe   seductress   clean of limit queen solid

of course i'm grown   receptacle for administrative
for talking points   a dent in inheritance in social
climber soundcloud google juicer   of course i'm not
stuck here in this box marked "log out"   just prefer
catastrophe to toy ducks   scapegoat to succubus
the anxiety of letting go of the handlebars to
pseudo-biological demon loving   of course i want

to move closer to the orchestra the possibility
of only one exit   because history carriages
and i didn't know it would be restorative to feel
self-conscious about my pulse   part of the ark
culture of a city in pairs   a way to transpose
track marks post post post   bench memories
into *of course women*   *don't dissolve or fly*

equipment aligns us   thanato-tour bus
death march mulch money even at the base
of this sycamore my focus on trucks men
walking cargo shorts tractors wife beaters
golf carts frustration   in robots admit
to commit myself to machines and water
a hesitation ground in the hyacinth
revoked   role-playing   fore farther

of course i make my home on the edge
of a park where we all see the woman
the atom hiding in constant transactional
analysis   a kind of *fear the beard* mantra
calling card   coquette   who hires reptiles
to reengage the unemployed   influential
dabblers   dapper in adjudicating self-
doubt   i know nuances are not as hard

as abbreviating akin to the gospel i learned
after first eating the apple   of course there's
charity in this moment where eve sees the leaf
as both elegant and contested   an allegory for
my discomfort   masks amphibians outcomes
inch out of this book and blurt my body is arbiter
a tangible response to imitation
                                                            the ground is your friend

INSTANT CLASSIC: think her

for/after Nicole Eisenman

1.

i used to think a woman
landless bargaining for scripture

ferocious comes only
in legend in the want

to keep away from produce
to reproduce the idea of one

direction trains coming concrete
end of the line let me

rip-off the clothes we disown
threadbare scenario in my gender

voluptuous philosopher dance
originally meant to be umbrella

of pine needles homage to
past tense thick metal mural

let me hold a facade of good
health a close reading of words

consume me opera propaganda

2.

i wish my forearm was as interesting
as fucking   the tattoo artist i don't
know   a frozen peach   i can't come
to terms   with mercury   cans   naked helps
quasi-eve looking   lilith solution a way
to reconcile my way out   of the garden
still speaking   more fluent   in tiara
in genocide   broke   in half   this epic
feels   a vast   container ship   stocked
with resentment   re-sentiment   i don't
think about proportion   tuna fish or
when it's time to exit   the rotunda
an evacuation party full of muscled thighs
styrofoam platters   will i ever have a "normal"
life   i never think to suss out   organizations
enrich through tallies of head lice   where
confidence wicks desire   i walk away learn
to sing and cry   the same time   profound
things   i cite them   incite as thunder employs
the paranoia instinct   this leak   on fire my
pillow a king-sized bed   ahead   of narrative
unavoidable   my memory play   i have a lot
of light cues   haloes   question awe detective
byline   hurricane photo booth pitstop porch
watch   roof lock   my thought bubble sees
what it means to be marked   affirm conversion
collate   "why are you apologizing this time?"

3.

i’m not as visible as you think i am   despite
the expelling expulsion mythographic version
where my hair pleases and i feel totally great
in humidity   humility a clause   a kind
of queen structure   fenced past   ringer
tee rhetoric of “i’m more than a rack and
a clock”   i’m not ashamed to never grow
up with friendship bracelets or autonomy
a lack of reference   lonely with a fan on

what if it’s a manicure that touched me
opened my face to see between a stranger’s
legs   what if this character learns to be sincere
takes a machine literally   misanthropic
sentimental   what if this character frames
pay stubs   lies down across commodification
arm wrestling   leg draped   storm clouds
gather me   anatomic vandal   what if this
character is tasteful in her ailment   shedding

skin emotionally liable   mood incongruent
i care what you make of dysregulation   my outbursts
come as specter   corrupt in pliant goggles
the common language of heretic   self-inflection
abdominal talking points   hyperrealism of
“i don’t know what we sprawl upon” what if
the figure drawing   reached out   sin-free
to welcome   elevated places   crowd scenes
unsoil me   commandment   figure   this

envy   active voice among ruins   too graphic
for the dragon   cherub   what if this picture

depicts graceful fig-leaf apron free ex post
facto sheer orchard vigor   leaf blood   what
ye conceal is not the mark of the beast
reprobate   not the flaming sword   rib
wrestler rather take thy seed and thy seed
and thy scene   unashamed   naked
head water   listen to the rabbit say

INSTANT CLASSIC : to know after

today feel a strange thing
the want to reappropriate
a story allow myself to stay
supplicant and revisit the land
i decline   an active verb
a decision marker   it isn't
the serpent who made me
it isn't the exile laryngitic
opus point where i lose
my voice and regain it
where i might accept
there's no clear road down
by the side of the mountain
because it's important
to rediscover the bath
ruins the scribe who rewrites
and rewrites   unaware
of all the glass walls all
man noise   deluge
all the instructions
of how to fill   the boat
with or without measuring
cups and an account
of all that advice i lost
somewhere between
the ol' genesis story
and this new history
i want to deploy with
all the nuance of
a lawnmower or that
special kind of inside
cycling where we pretend

to really just be
on a beach without
jellyfish or tacky lighting
when i sneeze i don't
mean to draw attention
to the space break my real
body requires   with or with
out loincloths an epic ceiling
ritual   it's true i cringe
at the thought of an island
or a farmhouse   a pickup
truck or a ladybug i'm not
one to permit entry via
man and security gate
moment of purity like
the week i did nothing
but memoir and my head
beat fitful as if all this
back story harbors purpose
as if i didn't lose my beauty
in the body i left behind
humor is not natural
and my idea of story
is this whole thing
a digression forgiven
by the intimacy of polytheism
byline kind   of disjointed
binoculars are the real weapon

INSTANT CLASSIC: moderately baroque

1.

"in the beginning was the war"[1]
in the beginning not an epigraph

or disclaimer–detect traces of fabric
trailers unruly   a way to own my own

ancestry   in the beginning i let the ducks
go by   repeat the word *disenchantment*

in the beginning we were at war we were
all just ordinary   form intent

on assimilating   a way to collate questions
like please   why apologize why rehabilitate

entitlement   a reference point for naming
with conviction   my cousins are always

among us   a revenue target set by
the hatches   that never open

1 from *After Such Knowledge* by Eva Hoffman

2.

in the beginning i didn't understand
robust in my abandonment

what it means to be in family both
inside and outside the double digit

pastoral gait   if you blush at autonomy
you'll always blush   in practical in practice

the promotion of *we are not finished* only
a precursor to law   a professionalizing

of robotic companionship phantom kitty
utterances   white-light experience of

the activist kind   technically silence
is a state of being forgotten

absence is the articulation of sand
on the edge of the garden scrawl

3.

in the beginning i notice the sound
of every sound the changing of locks

a blessing instead of poltergeist   rice
under control the way i give my play-

things room to survive what's not in
paper wall hanging   narration

of mouse pad antics   clear   assertive
scripture   can't savior you in the

beginning i wear a ukulele   name
my tendonitis   *ancient site* trim

my bangs build an assessment
of what we do with our bodies with

out dramatizing or formal terms
like *I should've been a cowboy* or

4.

let's rewrite plaques for a reason
let's take up all the space left on our

communal forearm maker-bot bust
because i talk myself into take myself

into the traditional dove trope i rationalize
as manifestation of my need for messengers

and rodents   pacifism and heaps of garbage
rat's nests of awesome congress   contact

designate   a parallel cinderella
useful in her treatment of the verb

"overcompensate"   nightfall   fertility
i don't have any hobbies   outside

of scarring   subtitle labels with epigraphs
of my grime   of my let's take on

5.

the cricket playhouse   the pantene
enigma   drawbridge party   wig stack

i spend too much on staph inflections
metered worry   look in the mirror

see the word “overwhelm”   remember
you were once a person without bronchitis

once a body outside of the rainbow flag
and the scab didn’t define me   once

i know sunday   i don’t rest   regret sweat
come out with sports caps   plastic dogs

say “when will the epic end”   realize
infirmary a bridge   a way into refrain

unknowing refusal to face the face of
our garden   all we care about is clothes

INSTANT CLASSIC: on contingence

at this point i don't care
about elevators or conversation
a shopping bag brings   the mark
on my arm   finally   heals   ceases
to be constant   activity transitions
to rote implied liability   deliver
my subset   at this point i happen
or not   fill ambience with acts
recopy   obvious chemistry   table
deals   vowels overbearing   at this
point i decide to assign bullets i want
to disembody him   it's topical
like "what's keeping you up at night"
or "thank you I hope that felt safe"

big business briefcasings underscore
man's original "what about me" mantra
its crescendo cellspace faux staccato
turn apple to mango then giraffe
then why   am i not surprised
by bombings or circumcision
at this point   my interest in sand
dry heat nosebleeds   man made
needles   at this point the buzz
a chainsaw my window i'm connected
to glass more than oxygen   body
mass more than hormones   positive
pressure monger tank respriational is it
wrong to just want to feel literal safe

toxic parts and toxins   my body
needs vacuum carrot caraway leeks

loincloth trouser dance i don't mean
to be indecent or exotic i am a man
who fashions flesh as more suitable
than produce   potencies become mark
of defense   i'm too old to hide
inside this genie's bottle of common
anemia post punk shag there's no
record of what we did without visit
i'm climbing some stupid mountain
emeritus i tell him i could live here

Notes

Book I

"under long obedience tried" (Milton, *Paradise Lost*, Book 7)
"so sang the hierarchies" (Milton, *Paradise Lost*, Book 7)
"so many nobler bodies to create" (Milton, *Paradise Lost*, Book 8)
"she was exactly like her" (Gertrude Stein)
"this friendly condescension to relate" (Milton, *Paradise Lost*, Book 8)
"Art—always—requires visible unrealities" (Borges)
"It is the celestial ennui of apartments" (Stevens)
"I settle on some British theme, some old/Romantic tale, by Milton left unsung" (Wordsworth)
"Whose higher intellectual more I shun" (Milton)
"what misery th'inabstinence of Eve" (Milton, *Paradise Lost*, Book 11)
"let us return to real-life dialogue" (Bahktin)
"as any demand is frigid until desire, until neurosis forms in it" (Barthes)
"I believe I'm not unrehearsed in what you're asking" (*The Symposium of Plato*)
"she composes herself by talking back" (Mcbeth)
"How can we be sure, how can we tell, whether any utterance is to be classed as performative or not?" (Austin)
"in situations where "having something to say" can mean risking vilification" (Malinowitz)
"outside the sentence *whose excitation would not otherwise have been revealed*" (Freud)
"some natural tears they dropped, but wiped them soon" (Milton, *Paradise Lost*, Book 12)
"we are so made that we can derive intense enjoyment only from a contrast" (Freud)
"...some minimal fabric of care, some margin of giving and receiving, is essential to life in extremity" (Terrence Des Pres)

Book II

"having always longed to be one of those happy gays myself" (Bersani)
"What remains is the most matter-of-fact observation: it is not good to have no home" (Améry)
"this 'I' was the voice of no author in my house." (Joan Didion)
"only the inferior stars/had disappeared" (Wordsworth)
"Intermix/my covenant in the woman's seed renewed./So send them forth—" (Milton, *Paradise Lost*, Book Eleven)
"let the disaster speak in you" (Blanchot)
"the bitter memory/Of what he was, what is, and what must be" (Milton, *Paradise Lost*, Book Four)

"we continually explore for the *invisible power structure* behind the visible kings" (Buckminster Fuller)

"Perfect within, no outward aid require/And all temptation to transgress repel." (Milton, *Paradise Lost,* Book 8)

"I sometimes hold it half a sin/To put in words the grief I feel;/For words, like Nature, half reveal/And half conceal the Soul within." (from *In Memoriam*, Tennyson)

Book III

"The serpent duped me and I ate" (Genesis 2:14)

"The earth received her sentence as the element out of which rebellious and fallen man was formed." (*Midrash)*

"everybody suspects us or knows but nobody says anything about it" (Gertrude Stein)

"...there was history, and there were historical novels and so there was in a way war all the time." (Stein)

"something closer to the enactment of experience" (Eva Hoffman)

"in real life you can't edit her out" (Etgar Keret)

Recent & Selected Titles

• **Dear All** by Michael Gottlieb. 114 p. $14.95.
• **Vile Lilt** by Nada Gordon. 96 p. $14.95.
• **Flowering Mall** by Brandon Brown. 112 p. $14.95.
• **ONE** by Blake Butler & Vanessa Place.
Assembled by Christopher Higgs. 152 p. $16.95
• **Motes** by Craig Dworkin. 88 p. $14.95
• **Scented Rushes** by Nada Gordon. 104 p. $13.95
• **Accidency** by Joel Kuszai. 120 p. $14.95.
• **Apocalypso** by Evelyn Reilly. 112 p. $14.95
• **Both Poems** by Anne Tardos. 112 p. $14.95
• **Against Professional Secrets** by César Vallejo.
Translated by Joseph Mulligan.
(complete Spanish/English) 104 p. $14.95.

Roof Books are published by
Segue Foundation
300 Bowery • New York, NY 10012
Visit our website at seguefoundation.com

Roof Books are distributed by
SMALL PRESS DISTRIBUTION
1341 Seventh Street • Berkeley, CA. 94710-1403.
Phone orders: 800-869-7553
spdbooks.org